Playing the Frame Drum

Online Audio

by Bill Woods

Photos by **Carole Woods**

To Access the Online Audio Go to:
www.melbay.com/30390BCDEB

Audio Contents

1	Rhythm 1	17	Rhythm 17	33	Rhythm 33	49	Rhythm 49	65	Rhythm 65	81	Rhythm 81
2	Rhythm 2	18	Rhythm 18	34	Rhythm 34	50	Rhythm 50	66	Rhythm 66	82	Rhythm 82
3	Rhythm 3	19	Rhythm 19	35	Rhythm 35	51	Rhythm 51	67	Rhythm 67	83	Rhythm 83
4	Rhythm 4	20	Rhythm 20	36	Rhythm 36	52	Rhythm 52	68	Rhythm 68	84	Rhythm 84
5	Rhythm 5	21	Rhythm 21	37	Rhythm 37	53	Rhythm 53	69	Rhythm 69	85	Rhythm 85
6	Rhythm 6	22	Rhythm 22	38	Rhythm 38	54	Rhythm 54	70	Rhythm 70	86	Rhythm 86
7	Rhythm 7	23	Rhythm 23	39	Rhythm 39	55	Rhythm 55	71	Rhythm 71	87	Rhythm 87
8	Rhythm 8	24	Rhythm 24	40	Rhythm 40	56	Rhythm 56	72	Rhythm 72	88	Rhythm 88
9	Rhythm 9	25	Rhythm 25	41	Rhythm 41	57	Rhythm 57	73	Rhythm 73	89	Rhythm 89
10	Rhythm 10	26	Rhythm 26	42	Rhythm 42	58	Rhythm 58	74	Rhythm 74	90	Rhythm 90
11	Rhythm 11	27	Rhythm 27	43	Rhythm 43	59	Rhythm 59	75	Rhythm 75	91	Rhythm 91
12	Rhythm 12	28	Rhythm 28	44	Rhythm 44	60	Rhythm 60	76	Rhythm 76	92	Rhythm 92
13	Rhythm 13	29	Rhythm 29	45	Rhythm 45	61	Rhythm 61	77	Rhythm 77	93	Rhythm 93
14	Rhythm 14	30	Rhythm 30	46	Rhythm 46	62	Rhythm 62	78	Rhythm 78	94	Rhythm 94
15	Rhythm 15	31	Rhythm 31	47	Rhythm 47	63	Rhythm 63	79	Rhythm 79	95	Rhythm 95
16	Rhythm 16	32	Rhythm 32	48	Rhythm 48	64	Rhythm 64	80	Rhythm 80	96	Rhythm 96

1 2

Visit us on the Web at www.melbay.com — E-mail us at email@melbay.com

Table of Contents

Preliminaries

What is a Frame Drum?

A frame drum is a drum whose head is wider than its rim is deep. Most frame drums have only one head, but there are exceptions. Some, like the tambourine, riq, and pandeiro, have zils around the rim that jingle when they are played. The bendir has strings against the inner surface of the head that make a buzzing sound like a snare when it is played. The daf has metal rings attached to the inside of the rim that vibrate when the drum is played.

Photo 1 shows my current collection of frame drums. Some of them have heads made of animal skin and some of them have heads made of artificial materials. The one at the top left in the photo was used to make the recording that accompanies this book. It has a goat skin head and you can hear how its tone changes with temperature and humitity on different audio tracks.

Photo 1 *My current collection of frame drums*

Playing Frame Drums

There are many types of frame drums in the world and many different ways of playing them. My previous books, **Bodhran: the Basics** and **Bodhran: Beyond the Basics**, show how to play the bodhran (an Irish frame drum) using a stick. This book shows how to play a frame drum using the fingers of your left and right hands and several surfaces of your right hand. There are many other ways of playing frame drums.

A Note To Left-Handed Players

This book is written from the perspective of a right-handed player. If you are left-handed, you have spent your whole life adapting to a predominantly right-handed world, and I am confident that you know what to do to make these instructions work for you.

Holding the Drum

Begin by sitting in a chair with the drum resting on your left thigh and your left wrist resting on the top of the rim as shown in *photo 2*.

Photo 2 *Holding the Drum*

Basic Right-Hand Strokes

There are three basic right-hand strokes; the thumb stroke (**T**), the ring finger stroke (**R**), and the full hand stroke (**F**).

Thumb Stroke

This stroke uses the side of your thumb to strike the head of the drum near the rim. We will start with an exaggerated description of this stroke.

Begin by resting your thumb against the head as shown in *photo 3*. Rotate your forearm to move your thumb away from the head as shown in *photo 4*. This is the starting position for this stroke. Now, keeping your hand relaxed, rotate your forearm quickly so your thumb hits the head and bounces back to the starting position (see *photo 5* through *photo 8*).

Some people find it useful to think of the thumb as pulling the tone from the drum head as your thumb rebounds rather than thumping the drum head as your hand comes in. This is not a different way of doing the stroke, just a different way of thinking about it.

Photo 3 *Thumb resting on the head of the drum*

 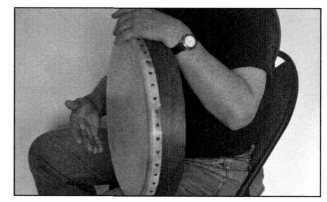

Photo 4 *Starting position for the thumb stroke*

 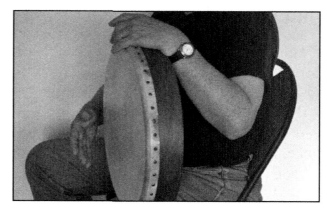

Photo 5 *The thumb halfway to the drum head*

Photo 6 *The thumb hitting the drum head*

Photo 7 *The thumb rebounding from the head*

Photo 8 *The thumb back in the starting position*

Notation

To indicate the thumb stroke, I use a capital **T**. To indicate equal periods of time in a rhythm pattern, I use a series of equal-sized rectangles. I put numbers over the rectangles so you can keep track of where you are in the pattern. The notation for a series of 8 equally-spaced thumb strokes is shown in *rhythm 1*, which you can hear played on *track 1* of the CD.

When *track 1* was recorded, the drum head was dry and tight. When you listen to *track 3*, you will hear how different the strokes sound on the same drum after the head has absorbed some moisture from the air. This is quite common with heads made of animal skin and is one reason some people prefer artificial heads. I prefer the feel and responsiveness of animal skin heads. You can decide for yourself which you prefer.

Track 1

1	2	3	4	5	6	7	8
T	T	T	T	T	T	T	T

Rhythm 1 Eight Thumb Strokes

Ring Finger Stroke

This stroke uses your ring finger to strike the drum right where the head passes over the rim. We will again start with an exaggerated description of the stroke. Begin by resting your ring finger on the head as shown in *photo 9*. Notice that this requires you to have your hand farther from the center of the drum head than for the thumb stroke. You should be able to feel the rim through the skin of the head. Rotate your forearm to move your ring finger away from the head as shown in *photo 10*. This is the starting position for this stroke. Now, keeping your hand relaxed, rotate your forearm quickly so your ring finger hits the head and bounces back to the starting position (see *photo 11* through *photo 14*).

As in the previous stroke, some people find it useful to think of pulling the tone from the drum as the ring finger rebounds.

 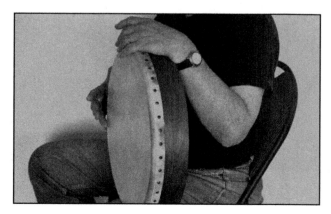

Photo 9 Ring finger resting on drum head where it passes over the rim

8

Photo 10 Starting position for ring finger stroke

 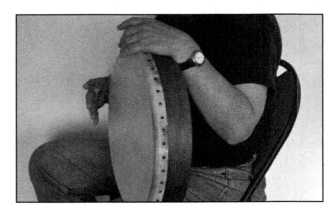

Photo 11 Ring finger halfway to the head

 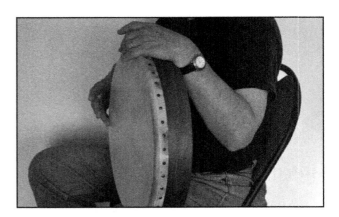

Photo 12 Ring finger hitting the drum head where it passes over the rim

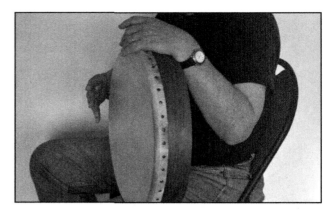

Photo 13 Ring finger rebounding from the drum head

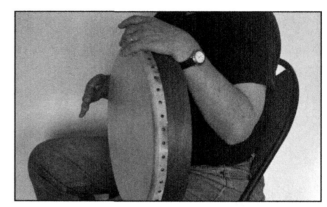

Photo 14 Ring finger back in starting position

More Notation

To indicate the ring finger stroke, I use a capital **R**. The notation for a series of 8 equally-spaced ring finger strokes is shown in *rhythm 2*. You can hear this played on *track 2* of the CD.

1	2	3	4	5	6	7	8
R	R	R	R	R	R	R	R

Rhythm 2 Eight Ring Finger Strokes

Alternating Strokes

As I mentioned earlier, the above descriptions are a bit exaggerated. If you are doing nothing but thumb strokes or ring finger strokes, they work fine, but if you are alternating between thumb strokes and ring finger strokes, you don't want to rebound all the way to the starting position after each stroke. That would take too much time and add unnecessary motion to your playing.

Rhythm 3 is alternating **T** and **R** strokes, and *photo 15* through *photo 20* show how it is played.

1	2	3	4	5	6	7	8
T	R	T	R	T	R	T	R

Rhythm 3 *Alternating Strokes*

Begin with your hand in the starting position for the thumb stroke (*photo 15*). Rotate your forearm so your thumb swings in and strikes the head an inch or so in from the rim (*photo 16*), but only rebound an inch or so (*photo 17*). Notice that your hand is now very close to being in the starting position for the ring finger stroke. As soon as your thumb rebounds, start moving your hand out toward the rim and rotate your forearm for the ring finger stroke (*photo 18*). Your ring finger should strike the head right where it passes over the rim (*photo 19*). Your hand should now be very close to the starting position for the thumb stroke. As soon as your ring finger rebounds from the drum head, start moving your hand back toward the center of the drum head (*photo 20*) for the next thumb stroke.

Photo 15 *Starting position for thumb stroke*

Photo 16 *Thumb hitting drum head*

 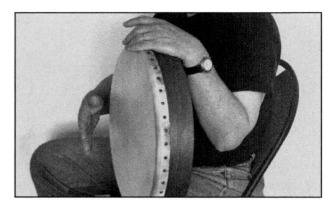

Photo 17 Thumb rebounding from drum head

 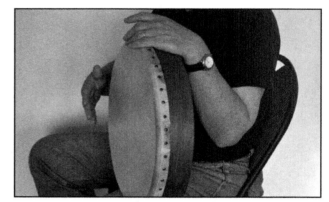

Photo 18 Hand moving to position ring finger over the rim

 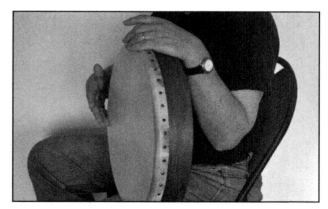

Photo 19 Ring finger striking drum head where it passes over the rim

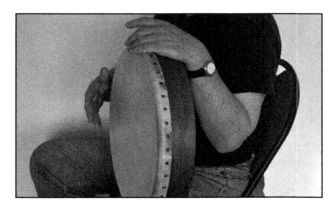

Photo 20 *Ring finger rebounding from the drum head*

All these detailed directions may make this seem more complicated than it actually is. Just try alternating between thumb strokes and ring finger strokes for a while without doing too much thinking about it, and it should start feeling very smooth and natural. Remember to move your hand toward the center of the head for the thumb strokes and back out to the rim for the ring finger strokes. Pay attention to the way the strokes feel and sound; make sure your thumb stroke produces a nice lower-pitched tone and your ring finger stroke produces a nice crisp high-pitched tone.

Full Hand Stroke

This stroke uses the palm of your hand and all five fingers. Hold your relaxed hand about five inches from the head near the center of the drum (*photo 21*). Now move your forearm toward the drum and plop your hand onto the drum head, making sure to keep everything relaxed (*photo 22*).

This stroke does not rebound. If it is to be followed soon by another stroke, you need to lift your hand off the drum head and prepare for the next stroke, but if there is some time before the next stroke, you can just leave your hand resting on the drum head for a while.

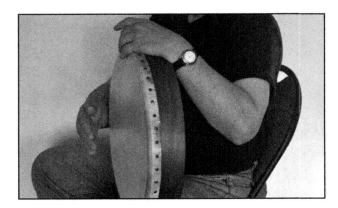

Photo 21 *Starting position for full hand stroke*

 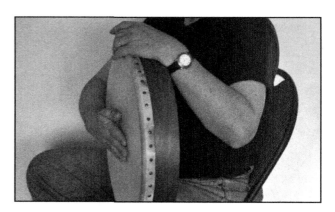

Photo 22 Full hand hitting drum head

More Notation

To indicate the full hand stroke, I use a capital **F**. *Rhythm 4* is eight equally-spaced full hand strokes.

Track 4

1	2	3	4	5	6	7	8
F	F	F	F	F	F	F	F

Rhythm 4 Eight Full Hand Strokes

On the CD, you can hear my hand lifting away from the head between the strokes. When you are playing lots of strokes, this sound will disappear into the background, but if you have an extended silence after an **F** stroke, I recommend leaving your hand on the head as long as you can before your next stroke.

Stroke Combinations

These are the three basic right hand strokes, so get used to playing them alone and in combinations. *Rhythm 5* through *rhythm 9* show some sample combinations to get you started.

Keep in mind that **R** is right on the rim, **T** is farther toward the center of the head, and **F** is at or very near the center of the head, so you need to keep moving the position of your right hand as you switch from one stroke to another. **R** strokes too near the center don't produce the crisp high-pitched tone we are trying for. **T** strokes too near the center of the head sound too mushy, and too near the rim, they don't produce the nice low tone we are trying to get. **F** strokes too near the rim ring too much and make your hand bounce, which will make it harder to control some of the strokes you will be learning later in the book. So, as you practice these patterns and the patterns you come up with yourself, don't forget to move your hand to the correct position for each stroke, and pay attention to how the strokes sound and feel.

1	2	3	4	5	6	7	8
T	R	T	F	T	R	T	F

Rhythm 5

1	2	3	4	5	6	7	8
T	T	R	R	T	T	F	F

Rhythm 6

1	2	3	4	5	6	7	8
T	R	F	R	T	T	F	R

Rhythm 7

1	2	3	4	5	6	7	8
T	T	F	R	T	F	R	F

Rhythm 8

1	2	3	4	5	6	7	8
T	R	F	T	T	F	R	F

Rhythm 9

Basic Left Hand Stroke

A Word of Encouragement

The basic left hand stroke is a ring finger stroke. Since most people don't use their left hand ring finger much, this stroke can be difficult to do, and it may take weeks or even months to develop a good strong left hand ring finger stroke – don't give up.

Getting into Position

First you need to get into the proper position for this stroke. Rest your wrist and hand on the rim so your relaxed fingers hang down, and have the end of your ring finger touching the drum head (*photo 23*).

Photo 23 Wrist and hand resting on rim

Now rotate your forearm so the end of your ring finger moves across the drum head to the place where the head passes over the rim (*photo 24*). You should be able to feel the rim through the skin of the drum head. This is where you want to hit the drum for this stroke.

Photo 24 Ring finger touching the rim through the drum head

Lift your ring finger away from the drum head (*photo 25*). This is the starting position for this stroke.

Photo 25 Starting position for ring finger stroke

Ring Finger Stroke

From the starting position, bring your ring finger down quickly so it hits the drum head right where it passes over the rim and then rebounds back to the starting position (*photo 26* through *photo 29*).

Photo 26 *Ring finger halfway to hitting drum head*

Photo 27 *Ring finger hitting the drum head where it passes over the rim*

Photo 28 *Ring finger rebounding from the drum head*

Photo 29 *Ring finger back in starting position*

More Notation

I use capital letters to represent right hand strokes and small letters to represent left hand strokes. A left hand ring finger stroke is represented by a small **r** to distinguish it from a right hand ring finger stroke, which is represented by a capital **R**. *Rhythm 10* is eight left hand ring finger strokes.

1	2	3	4	5	6	7	8
r	r	r	r	r	r	r	r

Rhythm 10 *Eight Left Hand Ring Finger Strokes*

Multiple Strokes per Rectangle

As I mentioned earlier, each rectangle in a given rhythm pattern represents an equal amount of time. So far we have had one stroke per rectangle, but it is quite common to have zero, two, three, or four strokes in a given rectangle. This does not change the length of time represented by the rectangle; it changes the speed at which the strokes in the rectangle are played.

For the sake of convenience, let's let one rectangle represent one second. If that rectangle contains no strokes, it represents one second of silence, although the overtones from a previous stroke may keep ringing during that "silence." If the rectangle contains one stroke, that stroke takes up one second. If it contains two strokes, each stroke takes up half a second. If it contains three strokes, each stroke takes up a third of a second. If it contains four strokes, each stroke takes up a fourth of a second.

Rhythm 11 is a progression from one stroke per rectangle to four strokes per rectangle.

1	2	3	4	5	6	7	8
T	T	T r	T r	T r R	r R r	T r R r	T r R r

Rhythm 11 One, two, three, and four strokes per rectangle

Rhythm 12 through *rhythm 14* show patterns with one, two, or zero strokes per rectangle. We will discuss three and four strokes per rectangle in later sections of the book.

1	2	3	4	5	6	7	8
T	R r	T	R	T r	R r	T	R

Rhythm 12

1	2	3	4	5	6	7	8
T	R		R	T	R r	R	

Rhythm 13

1	2	3	4	5	6	7	8
T	F r	T	R	T r	F r	T	R

Rhythm 14

Notice that the rectangles with two strokes in them start with a right hand stroke followed by a left hand ring finger stroke. This is very common, and you will see a lot of it in the upcoming rhythm patterns.

Middle Eastern Rhythms

This is not a book about Middle Eastern drumming, but the music from that part of the world provides a wealth of great rhythms, and I am going to take advantage of it.

A Bit About Middle Eastern Rhythms

In Middle Eastern music, rhythm is organized into cycles of beats and pauses. This concept of rhythmic cycles has different names in different regions; it is called *iqa'at* in many Arab countries.

Each rhythmic cycle has a name and consists of a fixed number and sequence of strong beats, weak beats, and silent beats. For our purposes, thumb strokes will be strong beats and right hand ring finger strokes will be weak beats. Despite what the terminology may imply, a weak beat is not quieter than a strong beat, it just has a different sound.

In performance, a rhythmic cycle will be enhanced by adding ornamentation and by filling in some of the silent beats with medium beats, but the underlying feel of the cycle is always maintained. For our purposes, full hand strokes and ring finger strokes (both hands) will be the medium beats used to embellish a basic rhythm.

Masmudi

There are many great Middle Eastern rhythms, and I will use one called masmudi to demonstrate some simple embellishments. This eight-beat cycle is named for the Masmud, a North African Berber tribe, and it is one of the most widely recognized Middle Eastern rhythms. *Rhythm 15* is the basic form of masmudi.

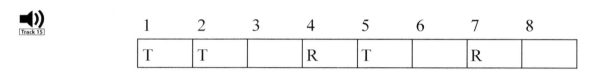

Rhythm 15 Masmudi, basic form

This basic form would almost never be played. It would be embellished in many creative and interesting ways. *Rhythm 16* and *rhythm 17* are simple embellished versions using the strokes that have been covered so far.

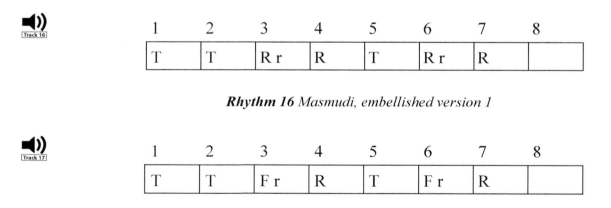

Rhythm 16 Masmudi, embellished version 1

Rhythm 17 Masmudi, embellished version 2

More Notation

Rhythm 18 shows one more notation convention. In rectangle 8, **Rr** is in parentheses. This means that this masmudi pattern is played through more than once, and the final **Rr** is played the first time through each repetition but not the second time. This is just a labor-saving device to avoid writing out a sixteen rectangle rhythm when the only difference between the first eight rectangles and the last eight rectangles is the absence of one or more strokes in the final rectangle, which is a very common occurrence. On the CD, *Rhythm 18* is played through four times; the final **Rr** is played on the first and third times through but not on the second and fourth times through.

1	2	3	4	5	6	7	8
T	T	F r	R	T r	R r	R	(R r)

Rhythm 18 Masmudi, embellished version 3

Rhythm 19 (not shown) is an extended performance of masmudi and can be heard on *track 19* of the CD. Notice how the underlying feel is maintained while the ornamentation adds variety to the rhythm. Experiment with creating your own ornamented versions of masmudi; it is a great rhythm to play around with.

Representing the Absence of a Stroke

I use a plus sign (+) to represent the absence of a stroke within a rectangle when it occurs in a place that is not obvious from the existing notation.

If a rectangle contains one stroke, but that stroke doesn't occur until halfway through the period of time represented by that rectangle, I put a plus sign in front of it, as shown in rectangle 1 of *figure 1*. This means that the period of time represented by that rectangle is divided into two parts, but there is no stroke in the first half.

1

+ r

Figure 1

This is demonstrated in *Rhythm 20*.

1	2	3	4	5	6	7	8
T r	+ r	+ r	+ r	T r	R r	R	(R r)

Rhythm 20 Rhythm with rests at the beginning of a beat

You now have all the tools you need to play and embellish the Middle Eastern rhythms in the next section. Have fun.

More on Middle Eastern Rhythm Cycles

Dum, Tek, and Ka

The goblet-shaped darbuka* is the main drum used in Middle Eastern music; and, like the frame drum, it has two main tones: a low-pitched tone called dum (rhymes with tomb), and a high pitched tone called tek (rhymes with wreck). These two tones are used to describe the strong and weak beats of a rhythmic cycle: a dum is a strong beat, and a tek is a weak beat. As I mentioned earlier, a weak beat is not quieter than a strong beat, it just has a different sound.

Tek and ka are used to distinguish a right hand tek (tek) from a left hand tek (ka), and there is a very nice system for describing and vocalizing Middle Eastern rhythms using dum, tek, and ka. Dum is usually abbreviated as D, tek as T, and ka as k.

There are many books and Internet sites with Middle Eastern rhythms written out using this dum tek ka system, and if the strokes we have learned so far were all the strokes we were going to learn, I would have used that system in this book. Unfortunately, the more advanced stroke combinations we will be discussing in later sections require a much more detailed system to describe them accurately, so I have chosen to use a notation system that tells you exactly which fingers or parts of the hand are needed for the different strokes.

To translate dum tek ka notation from another source into the notation used in this book, just replace dum with **T**, tek with **R**, and ka with **r**; and reverse the process to translate rhythms in this book to dum tek ka notation.

Look at hadrami, the first rhythm in this section. Using dum tek ka notation, it would be written DkTkDk. To vocalize this rhythm, you would say "dum ka tek ka dum ka," and when you play the rhythm, it will sound very much like the vocalization.

Names of Rhythms

As I mentioned earlier, each rhythmic cycle has a name. Some of the following rhythms have more than one name, and there are two reasons for this.

First, a given rhythm may have more than one name because it is played in different regions, and each region will have its own name for it.

---

* The names of drums from different cultures can be confusing. The Egyptian name for the darbuka is tabla. The Egyptian tabla should not be confused with the set of two drums from India which are also called tabla. An Egyptian tabla is a darbuka; the Indian tabla is something completely different. Also, because of its two main tones, the darbuka is sometimes called a dumbek in non-Arab countries, and dumbek sounds a bit like tombak, a Persian drum, but the tombak is again quite different in sound and playing style from the darbuka.

Secondly, a given rhythmic cycle played at different tempos may have different names for the different tempos. The feel the rhythm has when it is played slowly can be different from the feel it has when it is played fast, and this can affect when and how it is used. The rhythm called ayyub or zaar is a good example of this. When played fast, it is called ayyub and is used primarily in Sufi music and folk music. When played slowly, it is called zaar and is used for trance dances and for driving away evil spirits.

Another example of having different names at different tempos is the rhythm we have been referring to simply as masmudi. This is commonly done by drummers who are not from the Middle East, but in the Middle East, this rhythm is called masmudi kabir when it is played slowly (kabir is Arabic for "big" or "large"), and it is called masmudi saghir when it is played fast (saghir is Arabic for "little" or "small"). Masmudi saghir is also sometimes called baladi, which is Arabic for "country" or "people".

The following rhythms are just a small sampling from a rich and varied musical heritage. I have included cycles from three beats to ten beats. There are cycles of 24 beats and beyond, but I think the ones here will be enough to keep you busy for a while. As I mentioned earlier, there are many more rhythms available on the internet and in other books if you want to look for them.

Since no new strokes are introduced in these rhythms, they are not included on the CD. They are provided to help you get used to reading the notation, to let you practice combining the strokes you have learned so far, to let you practice ornamenting a given rhythm in different ways, and to introduce you to a bunch of great rhythms that you can add to your repertoire.

Hadrami

1	2	3
T r	R r	T r

Samai Ta'er

1	2	3
T		R

Mukhliss Jazaeri

1	2	3
T	T	R r

Ayyub or **Zaar**

1	2	3	4
T	+ r	T	R

Mukhliss Murakish

1	2	3
T	R r	

Bataihi

1	2	3	4
T	R	T	+ r

Samai Saraband

1	2	3
T	R	

Bembi

1	2	3	4
T r	+ r	T	R

Broll

1	2	3	4
T	+ r	R	R

Al Jird

1	2	3	4	5
T		R	R	

Fallahi

1	2	3	4
T	R	T	R

Batayhi

1	2	3	4	5
R r	T	R r	+ r	T

Malfuf or Wahda or Wahda Saghira or Laf

1	2	3	4
T	+ r		R

Massdar Iraqi

1	2	3	4	5
R	R	T	r T	+ r

Mokhliss Iraqi

1	2	3	4
T		R r	+ r

Mukhliss Murakishi

1	2	3	4	5
T	+ T		T	R

Saudi

1	2	3	4
T	+ T		R r

Arrdah Bahryah

1	2	3	4	5	6
T	T		T	R	

Wahda Mukallafah

1	2	3	4
T		R	R

Darij Jazaeri

1	2	3	4	5	6
T		R	R		T

Yemeni

1	2	3	4
T	R r	R	T

Darij Khaleeji

1	2	3	4	5	6
T	+ R		R	T	R

Aaraj or Aqsaq Turki or Thuryya

1	2	3	4	5
T		R		R

Darij Massri

1	2	3	4	5	6
T	R	T	R	R	

24

Farisah

1	2	3	4	5	6
T	R		R	R	

Samai Darj

1	2	3	4	5	6
T	R r	R	R	R	

Sinkin Samai or Yuruk Samai

1	2	3	4	5	6
T	R	R	T	R	

Dawr Hindi

1	2	3	4	5	6	7
T	R	R	T		R	

Nawakht

1	2	3	4	5	6	7
T		R	T		R	R

Qaimm Nussif

1	2	3	4	5	6	7
T	T	R	+ r	R	R	

Suffyan

1	2	3	4	5	6	7
T r		R	T r		R	R

Al Saut

1	2	3	4	5	6	7	8
T			R		T	R	

Al Saout Al Shami

1	2	3	4	5	6	7	8
T	+ r		R		R	T	R

Bataihi Muwassa

1	2	3	4	5	6	7	8
T	R r		R	R r		T	R

Batayha

1	2	3	4	5	6	7	8
T	+ r		R		T	R	

Chiftitelli

1	2	3	4	5	6	7	8
T	R r	+ r	R	T	T	R	

El Zaffa

1	2	3	4	5	6	7	8
T	R r	R	R	T	R	R	(R r)

Kata Kufti

1	2	3	4	5	6	7	8
T	R	R	T		R		R

Maqsum

1	2	3	4	5	6	7	8
T	R		R	T		R	

Masdar Leabi

1	2	3	4	5	6	7	8
T	T		R	T	T	R	

Masmudi Kabir or Masmudi Saghir or Baladi

1	2	3	4	5	6	7	8
T	T		R	T		R	

Masmudi Nusfi

1	2	3	4	5	6	7	8
T	T	T		T		R	

Mudawwar Saghir

1	2	3	4	5	6	7	8
T		R		T	T	T	

Muhajjar Turki

1	2	3	4	5	6	7	8
T	T	T		R		R r	R r

Mukhamass Arabi

1	2	3	4	5	6	7	8
T	R	T		R		R	R

Muthalith Iraqi

1	2	3	4	5	6	7	8
T	T	T	R	T		R	R

Qaimm Nussif Muwassa

1	2	3	4	5	6	7	8
T	+ r		R	R		R	R

Qatakufti

1	2	3	4	5	6	7	8
T	R	R	T		R		R

Saidi or Baladi Masri

1	2	3	4	5	6	7	8
T	R		T	T		R	

Sanaani

1	2	3	4	5	6	7	8
T		R	T		R	R	

Aqsaq

1	2	3	4	5	6	7	8	9
T		R		T		R		R

Awfar Mawlawi

1	2	3	4	5	6	7	8	9
T	R	R		T	T	R		R

Awnak Turki

1	2	3	4	5	6	7	8	9
T	R	R	T		R		R	

Dizikh

1	2	3	4	5	6	7	8	9
T	T	R r	+ r	+ r	T	T	R r	+ r

Karshlima

1	2	3	4	5	6	7	8	9
T		R		T		R	R	R

Jurjina or **Jurjuna**

1	2	3	4	5	6	7	8	9	10
T			R	T		R			

Mudawwar Shami

1	2	3	4	5	6	7	8	9	10
R		T		R		T	T	T	

Samai Aqsaq

1	2	3	4	5	6	7	8	9	10
T		T	R		T		R		R

Western Music Theory

In discussing Middle Eastern rhythms we talked about rhythmic cycles and strong, weak, and empty beats. The approach to rhythm in the so-called western world is a bit different, and I am going to start using some terms and concepts from Western music theory in the following sections, so we need to do a little re-framing. I don't think it will be as painful as it sounds.

Beats and Measures

In Western music theory, a piece of music is made up of measures, and each measure is divided into beats. *Figure 2* shows one measure that is divided into four beats. All the rectangles in the measure still represent equal periods of time.

1	2	3	4

Figure 2 One measure with four beats

Figure 3 shows two measures, each of which contains four beats. Notice that the number 1 at the beginning of each measure is in bold print; this is to make it easier to spot the beginning of each measure.

1	2	3	4	**1**	2	3	4

Figure 3 Two measures with four beats each

Notes and Rests

A period of sound is called a note, and a period of silence is called a rest.

Figure 4 shows the basic form of masmudi. If you play it, it will sound just like the basic form of masmudi in *rhythm 15*, but now we are describing it differently. Instead of an eight beat rhythmic cycle with strong, weak, and silent beats and a name, it is now a two-measure rhythm with notes and rests. The music is the same, but the terminology has changed.

Notice that the first beat of each measure in *figure 4* is in bold print. This is a second way to make it easier to spot the beginning of a measure. It is simply a visual aid, and bold notes are played the same as non-bold notes.

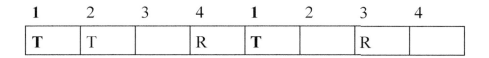

Figure 4 *Two measures with four beats each*

Quarter Notes and Quarter Rests

In *figure 4*, each note takes up one quarter of a four-beat measure, and each rest takes up one quarter of a four-beat measure. A note that takes up one quarter of a four-beat measure is called a quarter note, and a rest that takes up one quarter of a four-beat measure is called a quarter rest.

Tempo

Tempo is the speed at which a piece of music is played and is expressed in beats per minute. Most of the rhythms on the CD are played at slow or medium tempos so you can follow along with the notation, but as your skill level improves, you should try playing all of the rhythms at slow, medium, and fast tempos.

Divisions of the Beat

In *rhythm 21*, most of the beats contain two notes. These two notes are called divisions of the beat. Each division takes up one eighth of the measure, so these divisions of the beat are called eighth notes.

If you look ahead at *rhythm 22*, you will see that beat three of the first measure contains a plus sign and an **r**, which means the first half of that beat is a rest and the second half is an **r** stroke. In that measure, the plus sign is an eighth rest, and the **r** is an eighth note.

1	2	3	4	1	2	3	4
T r	F r	T	R r	**T** r	F r	T r	R (r)

Rhythm 21 *A four-measure rhythm pattern*

Syncopation

You have already been playing syncopated rhythms; we just haven't been calling them that.

If you look at the notation for *rhythm 21*, you will see that there is a note at the beginning of each beat. This sounds natural to us and is what we expect to hear.

If you look at beat three of the first measure of *rhythm 22*, you will see that there is a rest for the first half of the beat and a note for the second half of the beat. This shift of the note from the beginning of the beat to halfway through the beat is unexpected to our ears. This is called syncopation: the occurrence of rhythmic accents where they are not normally expected.

The only difference between *rhythm 21* and *rhythm 22* is the third beat of the first measure.

1	2	3	4	1	2	3	4
T r	F r	+ r	R r	**T** r	F r	T r	R (r)

Rhythm 22 *a four-measure rhythm with syncopation*

Longer Rhythms

So far the notation for a given rhythm has been printed on a single line. As we come up with longer patterns, the notation may need to expand to two or four lines.

Rhythm 23 is an eight-measure syncopated rhythm. The notation is four measures long, but the parentheses around the final **Rr** mean it should be played through twice with the final **Rr** omitted the second time through.

1	2	3	4	1	2	3	4
T	+ r	R	R	**T** r	+ r	R	R r

1	2	3	4	1	2	3	4
T	+ r	R	R	**T** r	R r	R	(R r)

Rhythm 23 *an eight-measure rhythm with syncopation*

Eight-Measure Rhythm Patterns

From now on, all rhythms will be played on the CD as at least eight-measures long. If the notation shows a two-measure pattern, that pattern will be played through four times. If the notation shows a four-measure pattern, that pattern will be played through two times. If the notation shows a pattern that is eight-measures or more, it will be played as written.

Syncopated Rhythms

Here are some syncopated rhythms for you to practice.

1	2	3	4	1	2	3	4
T	T r	F	+ r	T	T	+ r	F

Rhythm 24 *Syncopated rhythm*

1	2	3	4	1	2	3	4
T	T r	F	r T	+ T	+ r	F	(r)

Rhythm 25 *Syncopated rhythm*

1	2	3	4	1	2	3	4
T	T r	R	r T	+ T	+ r	R	(R r)

Rhythm 26 *Syncopated rhythm*

1	2	3	4	1	2	3	4
T r	+ r	F	T r	+ r	F	T r	R r

1	2	3	4	1	2	3	4
T r	+ r	F	T r	+ r	F	T	(R)

Rhythm 27 *Syncopated rhythm*

1	2	3	4	1	2	3	4
T r	F			T r	R r	+ r	+ r

1	2	3	4	1	2	3	4
T r	F			T r	R r	R	(R r)

Rhythm 28 *Syncopated rhythm*

1	2	3	4	1	2	3	4
T r	F r	+ r	R r	**T** r	F r	+ r	R r

1	2	3	4	1	2	3	4
T r	F r	+ r	R r	**T** r	F r	**T** r	R (r)

Rhythm 29 *Syncopated rhythm*

1	2	3	4	1	2	3	4
T	F	T	R r	**T** r	+ r	+ r	R

1	2	3	4	1	2	3	4
T	F	T	R r	**T** r	+ r	R	R r

1	2	3	4	1	2	3	4
T	F	T	R r	**T** r	+ r	+ r	R

1	2	3	4	1	2	3	4
T	F	T	R r	**T** r	+ r	R r	R (r)

Rhythm 30 *Syncopated rhythm*

1	2	3	4	1	2	3	4
T r	+ r	+ r	+ r	**T** r	F r	T r	F

1	2	3	4	1	2	3	4
T r	+ r	+ r	+ r	**T** r	F r	T	R r

1	2	3	4	1	2	3	4
T r	+ r	+ r	+ r	**T** r	F r	T r	F

1	2	3	4	1	2	3	4
T r	+ r	+ r	+ r	**T** r	R r	T	(R r)

Rhythm 31 *Syncopated rhythm*

1	2	3	4	1	2	3	4
T r	F r	T r	+ r	**R**	R r	T r	F r

1	2	3	4	1	2	3	4
T r	F r	T r	+ r	**R**	R r	T r	F

1	2	3	4	1	2	3	4
T r	F r	T r	+ r	**R**	R r	T r	F r

1	2	3	4	1	2	3	4
T r	F r	T r	+ r	**R**	R r	T r	R

Rhythm 32 *Syncopated rhythm*

Stroke Combinations

When playing eighth notes, you have already used the combinations **Tr**, **Rr**, **Fr**, and **rT**, which are played by alternating single right and left hand strokes. To allow us to play faster and more varied sequences, we will now learn some stroke combinations that use more than one finger per hand.

The mr Combination

This is where we add the left hand middle finger (**m**). As with **r** alone, this combination will probably take extra work because most people don't use their individual left hand fingers to do much, so those fingers are usually not particularly strong or coordinated. If this combination seems difficult, don't get discouraged – just keep practicing. It will be worth it.

Here is an exaggerated description of this combination. Put your left hand in a position similar to that for an **r** stroke but with **m** resting on the head where it passes over the rim as shown in *photo 30*.

Photo 30 **m** *on rim*

Lift **m** from the head as shown in *photo 31*. This is the starting position for this stroke.

Photo 31 **m** *lifted from head*

With **m**, strike the head right where it passes over the rim (*photo 32*).

Photo 32 **m** *striking the head*

Now bring **r** down to strike the head where it passes over the rim. As you are doing this, **m** should lift off the head, and your left hand should rotate a bit to follow the motion of **r**. This is shown in *photo 33* and *photo 34*.

Photo 33 **r** *moving toward the head*

Photo 34 **r** *striking the head*

This completes the **mr** combination, but as you move to whatever stroke you will be doing next, **r** should lift off the head of the drum in preparation for the next **r** or **mr** stroke.

The ultimate goal for learning these combinations is to increase your playing speed, but the combinations do not have to be played fast. *Rhythm 33* demonstrates some **mr** combinations played as quarter notes. This is a difficult combination for most people, so it is a good idea to start slowly. Try for a nice clean tone for both the middle finger and the ring finger.

1	2	3	4	1	2	3	4
T	m	r	F	**m**	r	T	(r)

Rhythm 33 quarter note **mr** *combinations*

Rhythm 34 and *rhythm 35* demonstrate some **mr** combinations played as eighth notes.

1	2	3	4	1	2	3	4
T	m r	R	m r	T	m r	R	(R)

Rhythm 34 eighth note **mr** *combinations*

1	2	3	4	1	2	3	4
T	m r	F	m r	T	m r	R r	R r

1	2	3	4	1	2	3	4
T	m r	F	m r	T	m r	R	(R)

Rhythm 35 eighth note **mr** *combinations*

Tmr, Rmr, and Fmr Combinations

These combinations put one of the main right hand strokes in front of an **mr** combination. *Rhythm 35* and *rhythm 36* demonstrate these combinations with three divisions to the beat. The naming convention for quarter notes and eighth notes is pretty logical, but when there are three divisions to a beat, the three notes that make up that beat are called triplets. I didn't make up the rules, I am just passing them on, so don't blame me.

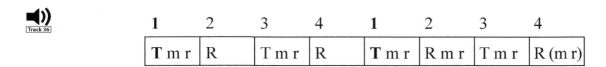

***Rhythm 36* Tmr** *and* **Rmr** *combinations as triplets*

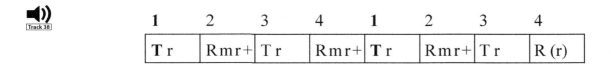

***Rhythm 37* Tmr, Fmr,** *and* **Rmr** *combinations as triplets*

Tmr+, Rmr+, and Fmr+ Combinations

Rhythm 38 through *rhythm 40* demonstrate these combinations with four divisions to the beat. At this point logic returns to our naming convention. Since each of these divisions takes up one sixteenth of a measure, the notes are called sixteenth notes, and the rests are called sixteenth rests.

1	2	3	4	1	2	3	4
T r	Rmr+	T r	Rmr+	T r	Rmr+	T r	R (r)

***Rhythm 38* Rmr+** *combinations*

1	2	3	4	1	2	3	4
T r	Tmr+	T r	Tmr+	T r	Tmr+	T r	R (r)

***Rhythm 39* Tmr+** *combinations*

1	2	3	4	1	2	3	4
T r	Fmr+	T r	Fmr+	T r	Fmr+	T r	R (r)

***Rhythm 40* Fmr+** *combinations*

The RI Combination

In the following description, **R** stands for the right ring finger, and **I** stands for the right index finger.

As usual we will start with an exaggerated description of this combination. As you get more comfortable with the motions involved, your finger movements should become faster and more economical.

First find a right hand position where both your ring finger and index finger rest easily on the head on or very near where the skin passes over the rim (*photo 35*). The relative lengths of ring fingers to index fingers vary from person to person, so a position that works for one person may not work for somebody else.

Photo 35 Right ring and index fingers touching the head near the rim

Now put **R** in the starting position shown in *photo 36*. Simultaneously rotate your right wrist and move **R** so it strikes the drum head on or near where it passes over the rim. **I** should now be an inch or two from the drum head (*photo 37*).

Now simultaneously rotate your right wrist and move **I** so it hits the drum head on or near where it passes over the rim. This should put **R** an inch or two from the drum head (*photo 38*).

This completes the **RI** combination, but as you move to whatever stroke will follow this combination, you should lift **I** away from the rim so it is ready when it is needed again.

As you are doing this combination, you rotate your forearm, but some of the action comes from moving your fingers as well, and keeping your hand and fingers relaxed is extremely important.

Photo 36 *Ring finger in starting position*

Photo 37 *Ring finger striking the head, index finger in position*

Photo 38 *Index finger striking the head*

Rhythm 41 through *rhythm 55* demonstrate the **RI** combination as eighth notes.

1	2	3	4	1	2	3	4
T	R I	r	R I	**r**	R I	r	(R r)

Rhythm 41 *eighth note* **RI** *combinations*

1	2	3	4	1	2	3	4
T	R I	r	T	**T**	R I	r	(R r)

Rhythm 42 *eighth note* **RI** *combinations*

1	2	3	4	1	2	3	4
T	m r	R I	r	**T**	r	R	(r)

Rhythm 43 *eighth note* **RI** *combinations*

1	2	3	4	1	2	3	4
T	r	F	r	**R** I	m r	R	(r)

Rhythm 44 *eighth note* **RI** *combinations*

1	2	3	4	1	2	3	4
T	r	R I	r	**R**	r	T	(r)

Rhythm 45 *eighth note* **RI** *combinations*

1	2	3	4	1	2	3	4
T	r	R I	r	**T** r	R I	m r	R (r)

Rhythm 46 *eighth note* **RI** *combinations*

1	2	3	4	1	2	3	4
T r	R I	m r	T r	**R** I	m r	T r	R (r)

Rhythm 47 *eighth note* **RI** *combinations*

1	2	3	4	1	2	3	4
T	m r	R	r	T	m r	R	r

1	2	3	4	1	2	3	4
T	m r	R I	r	T	r	R	(r)

Rhythm 48 *eighth note* **RI** *combinations*

1	2	3	4	1	2	3	4
T	m r	R I	r	T	m r	R I	r

1	2	3	4	1	2	3	4
T	m r	R I	r	T	r	R	(r)

Rhythm 49 *eighth note* **RI** *combinations*

1	2	3	4	1	2	3	4
T	r	F	r	T	r	R	m r

1	2	3	4	1	2	3	4
T	r	F	r	T r	R I	r	(R r)

Rhythm 50 *eighth note* **RI** *combinations*

1	2	3	4	1	2	3	4
T	r	F	r	T	r	R I	m r

1	2	3	4	1	2	3	4
T	r	F	r	R I	m r	R	

Rhythm 51 *eighth note* **RI** *combinations*

1	2	3	4	1	2	3	4
T	r	R I	m r	T	r	R I	m r

1	2	3	4	1	2	3	4
T	r	R I	m r	T	r	R	(r)

Rhythm 52 *eighth note* **RI** *combinations*

1	2	3	4	1	2	3	4
T	R I	m r	R	**R** I	m r	R I	m r

1	2	3	4	1	2	3	4
T	R I	m r	R	**R** I	m r	R	(r)

Rhythm 53 *eighth note* **RI** *combinations*

1	2	3	4	1	2	3	4
T r	R I	m r	R r	T r	R I	m r	R r

1	2	3	4	1	2	3	4
T r	R I	m r	R r	T r	R I	r	(R r)

Rhythm 54 *eighth note* **RI** *combinations*

1	2	3	4	1	2	3	4
T	r	F	r	**T**	r	R	m r

1	2	3	4	1	2	3	4
T	r	F	r	**T**	r	R I	m r

1	2	3	4	1	2	3	4
T	r	F	r	**T**	r	R	m r

1	2	3	4	1	2	3	4
T	r	F	r	**T** r	R I	r	

Rhythm 55 *eighth note* **RI** *combinations*

The RIr Combination

Rhythm 56 and *rhythm 57* demonstrate adding an **r** to the end of an **RI** combination to make some triplet combinations.

1	2	3	4	1	2	3	4
T	R I r	R	T	**R** I r	R I r	R	(T)

Rhythm 56 *Triplet* **RIr** *combinations*

1		2		3		4		1		2		3		4	
T m r		R I r		**T** m r		R I r		**T** m r		R I r		**T** m r		R	

Rhythm 57 *Triplet* **RIr** *combinations and* **Tmr** *combinations*

The RIr+ Combination

Rhythm 58 through *rhythm 60* demonstrate the **RIr+** combination as three sixteenth notes followed by a sixteenth rest.

1	2	3	4	1	2	3	4
T r	R I r +	R r	**T** r	**R** I r +	R r	**T** r	R (r)

Rhythm 58 **RIr+** *combination as sixteenths*

1	2	3	4	1	2	3	4
T r	R I r +	**T** r	R I r +	**T** r	R I r +	**T** r	R (r)

Rhythm 59 **RIr+** *combination as sixteenths*

1	2	3	4	1	2	3	4
T r	**T** r	+ r	+ r	**T** r	**T** r	R	R r

1	2	3	4	1	2	3	4
T r	**T** r	+ r	+ r	**T** r	R r	R (I r +	R r)

Rhythm 60 **RIr+** *combination as sixteenths*

The RImr Combination

You have already played this combination as eighth notes in the section on the **RI** combination. *Rhythm 61* demonstrates this combination played as sixteenth notes.

1	2	3	4	1	2	3	4
T r	**F** r	**T** r	R I m r	**T** r	R I m r	**T** r	R (r)

Rhythm 61 *Sixteenth note* **RImr** *combinations*

The UL Combination

Rather than multiple fingers, this combination uses the upper (**U**) and lower (**L**) parts of your right hand. Here is a detailed description of this combination.

Put your right hand in the starting position for an **F** stroke (this is shown in *photo 21* if you need to refresh your memory). It is very important to keep your hand relaxed when doing this combination, so make sure there is no tension in your hand. Rotate your forearm so the upper part of your hand hits the head of the drum as shown in *photo 39* and *photo 40*. Lift your hand slightly away from the head of the drum as shown in *photo 41*, and then rotate your forearm so that the lower part of your hand hits the head of the drum as shown in *photo 42* and *photo 43*.

Photo 39 *Upper part of hand halfway down*

Photo 40 *Upper part of hand striking the head*

Photo 41 Upper part of hand lifted off the head

Photo 42 Lower part of hand halfway down

 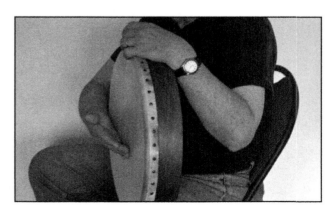

Photo 43 Lower part of hand striking the head

This completes the **UL** combination, but as always, you should lift the lower part of your hand off the drum head so your right hand is ready for whatever stroke is next.

Rhythm 62 through *rhythm 67* show some eighth note UL combinations.

1	2	3	4	1	2	3	4
T	F	U L	r	T r	R r	R I r +	R (r)

Rhythm 62 *Eighth note **UL** combinations*

1	2	3	4	1	2	3	4
T	r	U L	m r	T	r	R	(r)

Rhythm 63 *Eighth note **UL** combinations*

1	2	3	4	1	2	3	4
U L	m r	T	r	U L	m r	R	(r)

Rhythm 64 *Eighth note **UL** combinations*

1	2	3	4	1	2	3	4
T	F r	U L	r	T r	F r	U L	r

1	2	3	4	1	2	3	4
T	F r	U L	r	T r	F r	T	(R r)

Rhythm 65 *Eighth note **UL** combinations*

1	2	3	4	1	2	3	4
T	r	F	m r	T	r	U L	m r

1	2	3	4	1	2	3	4
T	r	F	m r	T	r	R	(r)

Rhythm 66 *Eighth note **UL** combinations*

1	2	3	4	1	2	3	4
T	r	U L	m r	T	r	U L	m r

1	2	3	4	1	2	3	4
T	r	U L	m r	T	r	R	(r)

Rhythm 67 Eighth note **UL** combinations

These are the basic combinations, but each of these combinations can be put together with another combination or with a single stroke to create combinations that might seem new but are just rearrangements or extensions of the combinations you already know. You will see some of this in the next section.

More on Syncopation

Syncopation is the occurrence of rhythmic accents where they are not normally expected. We have already learned that one way to do this is to put an eighth rest in the first half of a beat so the note doesn't come in until halfway through that beat.

Another way is to have an r for the first half of a beat followed by a **T**, **F**, or **U** for the second half of the beat. Our ears pick out the right hand stroke as more pronounced than the **r** and essentially slide the accent to the second half of that beat. **R** and **r** sound very much alike, but if you are careful to make the **R** louder than the **r**, this type of syncopation can also be done with an **rR** beat. *Rhythm 68* through *rhythm 78* demonstrate this type of syncopation.

1	2	3	4	1	2	3	4
T	r	F	r	T m	r F	m r	R (r)

Rhythm 68 Syncopation with an **rF** combination

1	2	3	4	1	2	3	4
T	r	R	r	T m	r R	m r	R (r)

Rhythm 69 Syncopation with an **rR** combination

1	2	3	4	1	2	3	4
T m	r R	m r	R r	T m	r R	m r	R (r)

Rhythm 70 Syncopation with **rR** combinations

1	2	3	4	1	2	3	4
T m	r R	m r	T m	**r** R	m r	T r	R (r)

*Rhythm 71 Syncopation with **rR** combinations*

1	2	3	4	1	2	3	4
T m	r T	m r	T m	**r** T	m r	T r	R (r)

*Rhythm 72 Syncopation with **rT** combinations*

1	2	3	4	1	2	3	4
T	F r	T m	r	**F** r	T m	r T	m r

1	2	3	4	1	2	3	4
T	F r	T m	r	**F** r	T r	R	(R r)

*Rhythm 73 Syncopation with an **rT** combination*

1	2	3	4	1	2	3	4
T	r	R I	r	**T** r	T m	r T	m r

1	2	3	4	1	2	3	4
T	r	R I	r	**T** r	R r	R	(R r)

*Rhythm 74 Syncopation with an **rT** combination*

1	2	3	4	1	2	3	4
T	r	R m	r	**T** r	U L	r U	L r

1	2	3	4	1	2	3	4
T	r	R m	r	**T** r	R r	T	(R r)

*Rhythm 75 Syncopation with an **rU** combination*

1	2	3	4	1	2	3	4
T	T r	R	R r	T r	T r	R	R r

1	2	3	4	1	2	3	4
T	T r	R	R r	T r	T m	r T	m r

*Rhythm 76 Syncopation with an **rT** combination*

1	2	3	4	1	2	3	4
T m	r T	m r	R r	T m	r T	m r	R r

1	2	3	4	1	2	3	4
T m	r T	m r	R r	T	r	R	(r)

*Rhythm 77 Syncopation with **rT** combinations*

1	2	3	4	1	2	3	4
T r	R I	r		T r	U L	r U	L r

1	2	3	4	1	2	3	4
T r	R I	r		T r	F r	T	(R r)

*Rhythm 78 Syncopation with an **rU** combination*

Simultaneous Strokes

This technique can be interesting if it is not over-used. It involves playing a right hand stroke and a left hand stroke at the same time and gives the impression that there are two drums playing instead of just one.

In *rhythm 79*, an **r** over a **T** or an **r** over an **R** means the two strokes should be played at the same time. This notation is awkward and takes up a lot of space, so I will give only one example, but you can play around with the concept and come up with your own rhythms if you want to.

1	2	3	4	1	2	3	4
r **T**	r T	r R	r R	**r** **T**	T r	R	r R

1	2	3	4	1	2	3	4
r **T**	r T	r R	r R	T r	T r	R	R r

1	2	3	4	1	2	3	4
T	r T	r R	r R	**r** **T**	T r	R	r R

1	2	3	4	1	2	3	4
r **T**	r T	r R	r R	**T** r	T	r R	

Rhythm 79 *Simultaneous strokes*

Three Beats Per Measure

Quarter Notes

Music with four beats per measure is by far the most common in Western music and is the standard we used to define quarter notes as notes that took up one beat of a four-beat measure. The good news is that we are going to keep the concept that a note that represents one beat is called a quarter note no matter how many beats there are in a measure.

So in *rhythm 80*, *rhythm 81*, and *rhythm 82*, a rectangle represents one beat, a note that takes up one beat is a quarter note, and we are still dealing with eighth notes, sixteenth notes and triplets. The only change is that there are only three beats per measure instead of four.

1	2	3	1	2	3
T	R m r	R	**T** m r	R	R

1	2	3	1	2	3
T	R m r	R	**T** m r	R	(R)

Rhythm 80 *Three beats per measure with quarter notes and triplets*

1	2	3	1	2	3
T r	F r	U L r +	T r	F r	U L r +

1	2	3	1	2	3
T r	F r	U L r +	T r	F r	R (r)

Rhythm 81 *Three beats per measure with eighth notes, sixteenth notes, and sixteenth rests*

1	2	3	1	2	3
T r	R I	r	T r	R I	r

1	2	3	1	2	3
T r	R I	r	**T**	R	R

1	2	3	1	2	3
T r	R I	r	T r	R I	r

1	2	3	1	2	3
T r	R I	r	**R**		

Rhythm 82 *Three beats per measure with quarter notes, quarter rests (at the end),*
and eighth notes

Odd Rhythms

Odd here does not mean strange or unusual, although these rhythms may seem that way at first. It simply means *not even*. For these rhythms, each measure will contain an odd number of divisions of the beat.

Odd rhythms are rare in standard Western music, but they are quite common in folk music from the Balkan countries. They take a bit of getting used to for most people, but once you get the hang of them, they are a lot of fun to play.

We have already looked at rhythm from the Middle Eastern and Western perspectives, and now we are going to look at it from the Balkan perspective. The main difference between the Balkan perspective and the Western perspective is that in Balkan music, the beats in a measure can represent different amounts of time – some beats are longer than other beats.

In order to explain these rhythms adequately, we need to make a small adjustment to the way we interpret our notation. Instead of a rectangle representing a quarter note, in these rhythms a rectangle will represent an eighth note.

Balkan folk dancers use the terms "quick" beat and "slow" beat when discussing dance rhythms. A quick beat is made up of two eighth notes, and a slow beat is made up of three eighth notes. A measure is generally made up of one or more quick beats combined with one slow beat, which results in an odd number of eighth notes per measure.

Fives

Look at *rhythm 83*. Each measure has two beats, one quick and one slow, for a total of five eighth notes per measure. The two eighth notes of a quick beat can be "counted" by saying "**Tah** Kuh" with emphasis on the **Tah**. The three eighth notes of a slow beat can be "counted" by saying "**Tah** Kuh Tuh" with emphasis on the **Tah**. I have indicated this by writing "**Tah** Kuh **Tah** Kuh Tuh" above the first measure.

There are two important things to remember about these rhythms. First, each eighth note in the rhythm still represents an equal amount of time; the beats may be different lengths, but the divisions of those beats are still all equal. Second, there is no pause between measures – there is a tendency for people used to "even" rhythms to pause for the length of an eighth rest at the end of an odd measure to make it come out even, so it may take a conscious effort to avoid doing this.

Listen to *track 83* of the CD and say or think "**Tah** Kuh **Tah** Kuh Tuh" along with each measure to get a feel for the rhythm. Once you are comfortable with the way it should sound, try playing along on your drum.

If you catch on to this rhythm quickly, that is great. If you have trouble, don't give up. Odd rhythms are initially difficult for most people, but they are a lot of fun and are worth the effort it takes to master them.

Tah	Kuh	**Tah**	Kuh	Tuh					
1		**2**			**1**		**2**		
T	r	T	m	r	T	r	R	m	r

1		**2**			**1**		**2**		
T	r	T	m	r	T	r	R	(m)	(r)

Rhythm 83 Odd rhythm with five eighth notes per measure

Sevens

The ruchenitsa is a Bulgarian folk dance that has two quick beats and one slow beat per measure for a total of seven eighth notes per measure. You can get a feeling for the rhythm by saying, "**Tah** Kuh **Tah** Kuh **Tah** Kuh Tuh." When played up to tempo, *Rhythm 83* through *rhythm 91* could be used to accompany a ruchenitsa.

Tah Kuh Tah Kuh Tah Kuh Tuh

1		2		3			1		2		3		
T		F		T		r	T	r	F	r	T	m	r

1		2		3			1		2		3		
T		F		T		r	T	r	R	r	T		(r)

Rhythm 84 Odd rhythm with seven eighth notes per measure

1		2		3			1		2		3		
T	r	F	r	U	L	r	T	r	F	r	U	L	r

1		2		3			1		2		3		
T	r	F	r	U	L	r	T	r	R	r	T		(r)

Rhythm 85 Odd rhythm with seven eighth notes per measure

1		2		3			1		2		3		
T		T		R	m	r	T	r	R	r	T	m	r

1		2		3			1		2		3		
T		T		R	m	r	T	r	R	r	T		(r)

Rhythm 86 Odd rhythm with seven eighth notes per measure

1		2		3			1		2		3		
T	r	F	r	F	m	r	T	r	F	r	F	m	r

1		2		3			1		2		3		
T	r	F	r	F	m	r	T	r	R	r	T	(m	r)

Rhythm 87 Odd rhythm with seven eighth notes per measure

53

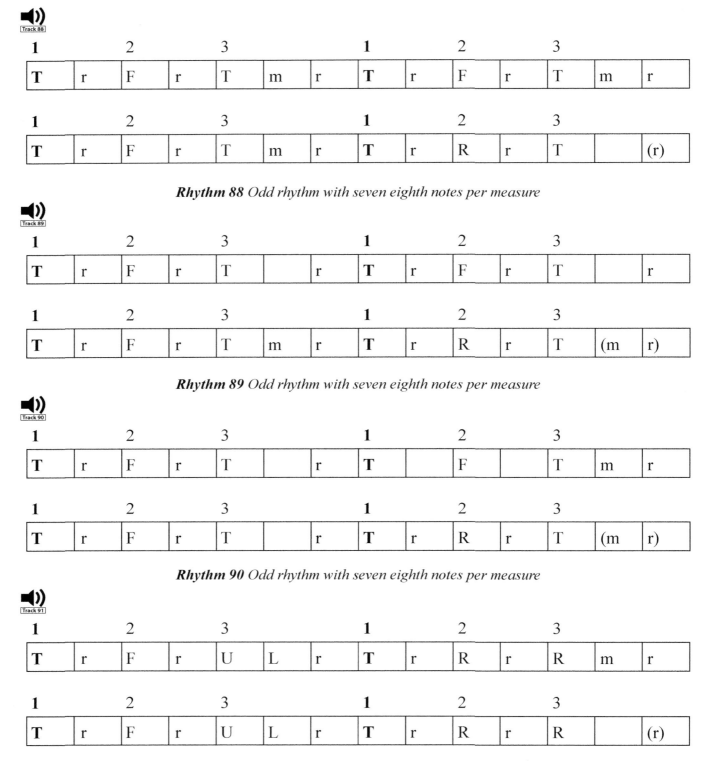

1		2		3			1		2		3		
T	r	F	r	T	m	r	T	r	F	r	T	m	r

1		2		3			1		2		3		
T	r	F	r	T	m	r	T	r	R	r	T		(r)

Rhythm 88 *Odd rhythm with seven eighth notes per measure*

1		2		3			1		2		3		
T	r	F	r	T		r	T	r	F	r	T		r

1		2		3			1		2		3		
T	r	F	r	T	m	r	T	r	R	r	T	(m)	r

Rhythm 89 *Odd rhythm with seven eighth notes per measure*

1		2		3			1		2		3		
T	r	F	r	T		r	T		F		T	m	r

1		2		3			1		2		3		
T	r	F	r	T		r	T	r	R	r	T	(m)	r

Rhythm 90 *Odd rhythm with seven eighth notes per measure*

1		2		3			1		2		3		
T	r	F	r	U	L	r	T	r	R	r	R	m	r

1		2		3			1		2		3		
T	r	F	r	U	L	r	T	r	R	r	R		(r)

Rhythm 91 *Odd rhythm with seven eighth notes per measure*

The lesnoto is a Macedonian folk dance that has one slow beat and two quick beats per measure, which still gives us seven eighth notes per measure, but having the slow beat at the beginning of the measure rather than at the end gives a different feel to the rhythm. *Rhythm 92* through *rhythm 96* could be used to accompany a lesnoto.

Tah Kuh Tuh **Tah** Kuh **Tah** Kuh

1			2		3		1			2		3	
T	m	r	T	r	R	r	T	m	r	T	r	R	r

1			2		3		1			2		3	
T	m	r	T	r	R	r	T	m	r	T		(R)	

Rhythm 92 Odd rhythm with seven eighth notes per measure

1			2		3		1			2		3	
T	m	r	R		R		T			R	r	R	r

1			2		3		1			2		3	
T	m	r	R		R		T			(R	r	R	r)

Rhythm 93 (CD track 93) Odd rhythm with seven eighth notes per measure

1			2		3		1			2		3	
T	m	r	R	r	R	r	T	m	r	R		(R)	

Rhythm 94 Odd rhythm with seven eighth notes per measure

1			2		3		1			2		3	
T	m	r	R		R		T	m	r	R	(r	R	r)

Rhythm 95 Odd rhythm with seven eighth notes per measure

1			2		3		1			2		3	
T		r	R		R		T	m	r	R	(r	R	r)

Rhythm 96 Odd rhythm with seven eighth notes per measure

The End

That's it for this book. I hope it has been helpful and that you enjoy many hours of drumming in the years to come.

Printed in Great Britain
by Amazon

15887124R00034

ABOUT THIS BOOK

Playing the Frame Drum

by Bill Woods

This book and accompanying audio show you how to play the frame drum using your fingers and hand surfaces. The method uses text, photographs, and the audio examples to demonstrate the various strokes and rhythms. Three ways of looking at rhythms are presented: Middle Eastern, Western and Balkan, with over 160 demonstrated rhythms. Includes access to an online audio recording.

Toll Free 1-800-8-MEL BAY (1-800-863-5229)
Fax (636) 257-5062
email@melbay.com

www.MELBAY.com

ISBN 978-078-669-582-9

$19.99

MB30390M
$19.99 USD

9 780786 695829

51999